Introduction

"Delicious Pasta Recipes for Kids" is a fantastic cookbook that aims to bring the joy of pasta to young chefs in a fun and flavorful way. With its collection of delectable recipes, this cookbook is designed to inspire children to explore the wonders of pasta while developing their culinary skills.

Inside these pages, you'll find a treasure trove of pasta recipes specifically tailored to suit the tastes and preferences of kids. From creamy and cheesy macaroni to zesty tomato-based dishes, the recipes in this cookbook offer a wide range of flavors and ingredients that will satisfy even the pickiest of eaters.

Each recipe is thoughtfully crafted with easy-to-follow instructions, ensuring that children can actively participate in the cooking process with confidence. The cookbook also includes vibrant and enticing visuals that will captivate young readers, igniting their enthusiasm for cooking and encouraging their creativity in the kitchen.

Not only does "Delicious Pasta Recipes for Kids" focus on making meals that taste great, but it also places an emphasis on using nutritious ingredients. The cookbook provides helpful tips on incorporating vegetables, lean proteins, and whole grains into pasta dishes, promoting a balanced and wholesome approach to eating.

With this cookbook, children will not only discover the pleasure of preparing their own meals but also develop valuable life skills, such as following recipes, measuring ingredients, and understanding cooking techniques. They will gain a sense of accomplishment as they serve up delicious and satisfying pasta dishes to their family and friends.

"Delicious Pasta Recipes for Kids" is more than just a cookbook; it's a gateway to a world of culinary adventure and creativity. It invites children to embark on a flavorful journey where they can learn, experiment, and, most importantly, enjoy the wonderful world of pasta. Whether your child is a pasta lover or a budding chef, this cookbook is the perfect companion for making mealtimes a joyous and delicious experience.

Sausage Pasta

Ingredients

1 tbsp olive oil.
packet of 8 pork sausages (the best your budget will allow), cut into chunky pieces.
1 large onion, chopped.
2 garlic cloves, crushed.
1 tsp chilli powder.
400g can chopped tomatoes.
300g short pasta such as fusilli or farfalle (just over half a 500g bag)

This delicious sausage pasta recipe is perfect for kids who are just starting to learn how to cook. All you need is a few simple ingredients and about 30 minutes of your time. Heat the olive oil in a large frying pan, then add the sausages, onion and garlic and fry until lightly browned. Add the chilli powder, tomatoes and pasta, then cook for 15-20 minutes, stirring occasionally. Serve with some freshly grated Parmesan and garlic bread, if desired. This delicious sausage pasta is sure to be a hit with the kids! Try using different types of sausages or adding in other vegetables like peppers or mushrooms to make it even more delicious. With this easy recipe, you'll be able to whip up delicious meals for your kids in no time. Enjoy!

Creamy Salmon Pasta Bake

Ingredients
1 pack of J James salmon pieces - we used 356g.
400 g pasta - we used Spirali.
2 leeks.
2 cloves of garlic - minced.
1 handful of parsley.
1 handful of mint.
1 tbsp wholegrain mustard.
25 g butter.

If you're looking for delicious recipes to cook with your kids, this creamy salmon pasta bake is a great choice. It's simple to make and full of flavor!

To start, preheat your oven to 200°C / Fan 180°C / Gas Mark 6 and lightly grease an oven-proof dish. Then, in a pan, cook the salmon pieces until they're cooked through.

Next, cook the pasta in a large saucepan with boiling water according to packet instructions. Once it's done cooking, drain and set aside.

In another pan, melt the butter before adding the leeks and garlic and cooking for 3-4 minutes until softened. Then, add the cooked salmon pieces, parsley, mint and wholegrain mustard. Mix together before adding the pasta and stirring until everything is evenly combined.

Finally, spoon the delicious creamy salmon pasta bake into your oven-proof dish and cook for 15-20 minutes until golden brown on top. Enjoy!

Tuna Pasta Bake

This delicious tuna pasta bake is a great way to get kids involved in cooking delicious meals. Preparing the ingredients is easy and straightforward, so it's perfect for beginners. To begin, preheat your oven to 200°C/fan 180°C/gas 6. Boil 300g of fresh egg penne according to packet instructions. In a large bowl, mix together 500g of tomato and herb pasta sauce with three 120g tins of tuna steak in springwater (drained and flaked). Add 325g tin of sweetcorn in water (drained), 390g carton Italian chopped tomatoes, 14g fresh flat-leaf parsley leaves (picked, washed and chopped) and stir everything together.

Tip the pasta into a large ovenproof dish and top with the tuna mixture. Sprinkle over 100g of grated mature cheddar cheese and bake in the preheated oven for 25-30 minutes, until golden brown on top and bubbling around the edges. Enjoy your delicious tuna pasta bake, and don't forget to save some leftovers for the next day. Bon appetite!

This delicious recipe is sure to be a hit with kids of all ages, so why not get them involved in cooking it? Get your little ones chopping, stirring and sprinkling cheese - they will feel proud of their delicious accomplishment when it comes out of the oven! Enjoy your delicious tuna pasta bake with your family and friends. Happy cooking!

Cheesy Ham And Broccoli Pasta

Ingredients

1 head of broccoli, cut into small florets.
1 tbsp oil.
1 onion, finely chopped.
2 garlic cloves, crushed.
250g ham, cut into chunks (get a nice thick slice from the deli counter)
300ml pot double cream.
1 tbsp English mustard.

This delicious cheesy ham and broccoli pasta dish is the perfect meal to make for your family, especially if you have young children! It's an easy-to-make recipe that has plenty of flavor and is sure to become a family favorite. To start, heat the oil in a large frying pan over medium heat. Add the chopped onion, garlic and ham and cook for 5 minutes until the vegetables are softened. Then, add the broccoli florets and cook for a further 3-4 minutes. Once the vegetables are cooked, pour in the double cream and mustard and stir together to combine. Allow it to simmer gently for 10 minutes before adding grated cheese of your choice (we recommend cheddar or mozzarella). Once the cheese is melted, turn off the heat and season with salt and pepper to taste. Serve over your favorite cooked pasta noodles and enjoy! With this delicious recipe, your kids will be begging for seconds in no time!

Pesto Salmon Pasta Bake

Ingredients
350g penne.
2 x 212g tins pink salmon, drained.
1 lemon, zested and juiced.
190g jar green pesto.
250g pack cherry tomatoes, halved.
100g bunch spring onions, finely sliced.
125g pack reduced-fat mozzarella.

This delicious pesto salmon pasta bake makes for a delicious and healthy meal that kids will love! With only a few simple ingredients, you can whip up this delicious dish in no time.

To start with, preheat your oven to 200°C/gas mark 6. Then grab a large pot and cook your penne according to the packet instructions. Once cooked, drain the penne and transfer to an ovenproof dish.

Next, mix together the canned salmon with the lemon zest and juice. Spread this mixture over the cooked penne in the dish and stir everything together. Then spread over your delicious green pesto sauce followed by halved cherry tomatoes and sliced spring onions. Finally, top with the reduced-fat mozzarella and pop it into your preheated oven for 20 minutes until golden and bubbling.

This delicious pesto salmon pasta bake is so easy to make and will quickly become a family favorite! And as an added bonus, it's super healthy too thanks to all the delicious, fresh ingredients. So why not try it for dinner tonight and treat your family to a delicious and nutritious meal! Enjoy!

Quick And Easy Pasta Salad

Making delicious pasta salad recipes at home can be an easy and fun activity to do with the kids. Follow these simple steps to learn how to cook a delicious pasta salad in no time.

You will need: 1 (16 ounce) package uncooked rotini pasta, 1 (16 ounce) bottle Italian Salad Dressing, 2 cucumbers, 6 tomatoes, 1 bunch green onions, 4 ounces grated Parmesan cheese and 1 tablespoon Italian seasoning.

Begin by boiling the rotini pasta according to package instructions. Once cooked, drain the pasta and allow it to cool down. While the pasta is cooling, chop up 2 cucumbers, 6 tomatoes and 1 bunch of green onions. Place the vegetables in a large bowl.

Once the pasta has cooled, add it to the vegetables and stir until everything is mixed together. Pour 1 (16 ounce) bottle of Italian Salad Dressing over the mixture and sprinkle 1 tablespoon of Italian seasoning on top. Stir everything together again and then garnish with 4 ounces of grated Parmesan cheese.

Your delicious pasta salad is now ready to serve! Enjoy this delicious recipe with your kids and their friends.

Tip: You can also add other vegetables, meat or seafood of your choice to the pasta salad to make it even more delicious! Try adding in some bell peppers, olives, ham or shrimp for a delicious twist. Experiment with different flavors to create your own delicious recipes!

Happy cooking! :)

Chicken Pasta Bake

Ingredients
4 tbsp olive oil
1 onion, finely chopped
2 garlic cloves, crushed
¼ tsp chilli flakes
2 x 400g cans chopped tomatoes
1 tsp caster sugar
6 tbsp mascarpone
4 skinless chicken breasts, sliced into strips
300g penne
70g mature cheddar, grated
50g grated mozzarella
½ small bunch of parsley, finely chopped!

Make delicious meals for your kids with this easy-to-follow chicken pasta bake recipe. Begin by preheating the oven to 200°C/ 180°C fan/ gas mark 6. Then, heat 2 tablespoons of olive oil in a large saucepan over a medium heat and add the chopped onion, garlic cloves and chilli flakes. Cook for 5-7 minutes until softened, stirring occasionally.

Add the chopped tomatoes and caster sugar to the pan and bring to a simmer over a medium-high heat. Simmer for about 10 minutes, stirring occasionally until thickened. Add the mascarpone and stir until melted into the tomato sauce.

Heat 2 more tablespoons of olive oil in a separate large saucepan over a medium-high heat. Add the sliced chicken and cook for 5-7 minutes until golden and cooked through, stirring occasionally.

Meanwhile, cook the penne in boiling salted water according to the packet instructions until just al dente. Drain well.

Add the cooked chicken to the tomato sauce and stir to combine. Add the cooked penne, grated cheddar and mozzarella and chopped parsley, season with salt and black pepper, then stir until evenly combined.

Transfer the chicken pasta bake mixture to an ovenproof dish, cover with foil and bake for 20 minutes until bubbling. Remove the foil and bake for a further 5 minutes until the cheese is golden and melted. Serve hot. Enjoy!

Creamy Mushroom Pasta

Creating delicious recipes for kids is easy to do with creamy mushroom pasta. This delicious dish makes a great meal that the whole family will enjoy. To make this delicious meal all you need are 8 ounces of fettuccine, 2 tablespoons of olive oil, ¾ pound of fresh white mushrooms (sliced), ¼ pound of fresh shiitake mushrooms (stemmed and sliced), salt and ground black pepper to taste, 2 cloves of garlic (minced), 2 fluid ounces of sherry and 1 cup of chicken stock.

To begin cooking this delicious dish, start by boiling the fettuccine in a large pot for about 8 minutes or until it's al dente. Once cooked, drain the pasta and set aside.

Next, heat a large skillet over medium-high heat and add in the olive oil. Once heated, add in the mushrooms and sauté them until they are lightly browned (about 5 minutes). After this step, season with salt and pepper to taste.

Then, add in the garlic and sauté for another minute before adding in the sherry. Allow the sherry to cook until it is almost completely evaporated. Finally, pour in the chicken stock and bring the mixture to a boil. Once all ingredients are incorporated, reduce heat to low and simmer until the sauce has thickened (about 8-10 minutes).

When the sauce is finished simmering, add in the cooked pasta and mix together until all ingredients are combined. Serve this delicious creamy mushroom pasta with a side of fresh parmesan cheese. Enjoy!

This delicious creamy mushroom pasta recipe is sure to be a hit with your kids. Its delicious flavor and simple ingredients make it an easy meal to whip up for a delicious family dinner. Enjoy!

Chicken And Creamy Bacon Penne

Ingredients

1 tbsp olive oil.
2 boneless skinless chicken breasts.
100g smoked lardon (chopped bacon)
4 tbsp dry white wine.
100g frozen petits pois.
5 tbsp double cream.
8220g packet cooked penne.!

Chicken with creamy bacon penne is a delicious recipe for kids that's easy to cook. Begin by heating the olive oil in a large non-stick pan and adding the chicken breasts. Cook these until golden brown, then add the chopped lardon (bacon) and fry until crisp. Next, pour in the white wine, stirring continuously to prevent sticking. Once the wine has reduced by half, add in small handfuls of frozen petits pois and stir until cooked through.

Finally, reduce to a low heat and add in the double cream and cooked penne. Stir continuously for 4-5 minutes until all ingredients are combined and creamy sauce is formed. Serve hot for delicious family meal. Enjoy!

Baked Feta Pasta

ingredients

2 pints (20 oz) grape tomatoes.
1/2 cup extra-virgin olive oil.
Salt and freshly ground black pepper.
7 oz. block feta cheese (sheep's milk variety), drained.
10 oz. dry pasta (bite size)
5 medium garlic cloves, peeled and halved.
8 oz. ...
1/4 tsp crushed red pepper flakes, or more to taste.

Baked Feta Pasta is an easy and healthy dish that takes only minimal time to prepare. With just a handful of simple ingredients, you can create this delicious meal. To make it, start by preheating your oven to 425 degrees Fahrenheit.

In a large bowl, combine the grape tomatoes, extra-virgin olive oil, salt and pepper. Cut the feta cheese into small cubes and add it to the bowl. Next, cook 10 oz of bite-size pasta according to package instructions until al dente. Once done, drain it and mix it with the tomato mixture in the bowl.

Add garlic cloves, 8 oz of mushrooms (sliced), and 1/4 tsp of crushed red pepper flakes, or to taste. Toss everything together and spread it in a single layer on an oven-safe dish. Bake for 25 minutes until the top is lightly golden brown.

Baked Feta Pasta is now ready to enjoy! Serve with a sprinkling of fresh herbs, extra olive oil, and a side of crusty bread. This healthy pasta dish makes for a great weeknight dinner that is sure to please the whole family. Enjoy!

Fettuccine Alfredo

Ingredients

1 pound fettuccine noodles (use gluten-free, legume, or zucchini noodles if desired)
4 garlic cloves.
1 small head cauliflower (1 1/2 to 2 pounds), enough for 6 cups florets.
4 tablespoons olive oil.
1 cup raw unsalted cashews.
2 cups vegetable broth.
⅛ teaspoon onion powder.
1/8 + ¼ teaspoon ground black pepper.

ettuccine Alfredo is a healthy pasta dish that you can easily prepare in the comfort of your own home. To make this healthy version, start by boiling the fettuccine noodles according to package instructions. Meanwhile, mince the garlic cloves and cut the head of cauliflower into florets. Heat olive oil in a pan and add the garlic and cauliflower florets. Cook until the cauliflower is tender, stirring occasionally. In a high-speed blender, add the cashews, vegetable broth, onion powder, and black pepper and blend on high speed until smooth. Pour the sauce over the cooked fettuccine noodles and mix to combine. Serve warm and enjoy! With this healthy pasta dish, you can have a delicious meal that's sure to please. Bon Appetit!

Goat Cheese Spinach Pasta

Ingredients

8 ounces uncooked pasta.
4 ounces goat cheese crumbled.
1/2 cup freshly grated parmesan cheese.
1 teaspoon fresh lemon juice.
1 tablespoon butter.
1 clove garlic minced.
2 cups fresh baby spinach (packed)
1 tablespoon chopped fresh basil (optional)

This healthy pasta dish is easy to make and incredibly flavorful. It combines the tangy flavor of goat cheese with the earthy taste of spinach, all tossed in a light lemon butter sauce.

To prepare, begin by bringing a pot of salted water to a boil over high heat. Add the pasta and cook for 8-10 minutes until al dente.

Meanwhile, melt the butter in a large skillet over medium heat. Add the garlic and sauté for one minute, then reduce the heat to low and add the spinach. Cook until wilted and tender, about 3-4 minutes.

Add the cooked pasta to the skillet with the spinach, stirring to combine. Add the goat cheese and parmesan, stirring until melted. Finally, stir in the lemon juice and season with salt, pepper, and fresh basil (if using). Serve warm.

This healthy pasta dish is a great way to get your dose of greens while still indulging in comfort food. Enjoy!

Ricotta Pasta

Ingredients

12 ounces bucatini or spaghetti.
1 cup ricotta cheese.
1 tablespoon olive oil.
½ cup grated Parmesan cheese, plus more to garnish.
½ teaspoon kosher salt.
Fresh ground black pepper.
Zest of 1 lemon (plus reserve some for garnish)
¼ cup pasta water.

This healthy pasta dish combines classic Italian flavors with the deliciousness of ricotta cheese. The result is a healthy but hearty meal that you can prepare in just 30 minutes. To make ricotta pasta, start by boiling 12 ounces of bucatini or spaghetti according to package directions and reserving ¼ cup of the cooking liquid before draining. In a large skillet, heat one tablespoon of olive oil over medium-high heat. Add the cooked pasta and ¾ cup ricotta cheese and stir until it's well combined. Sprinkle with ½ teaspoon kosher salt and a few grinds of black pepper. Add the grated Parmesan cheese, lemon zest and reserved cooking liquid to the skillet and stir to incorporate. Serve with extra Parmesan cheese and lemon zest for garnish. Enjoy this healthy pasta dish as a quick, easy weeknight meal or serve it as part of a special occasion dinner. Bon Appetit!

Spinach Mascarpone Lasagne

Ingredients
400g spinach.
1 tbsp olive oil.
2 garlic cloves, crushed.
250g mascarpone.
1 tsp ground nutmeg.
100g parmesan (or vegetarian alternative), grated.
9 lasagne sheets.
100ml double cream.

This healthy spinach and mascarpone lasagne is a delicious pasta dish that's easy to prepare. Start by preheating the oven to 200C/180C fan/gas 6. Then, heat 1 tablespoon of olive oil in a large saucepan over medium heat. Add 2 crushed garlic cloves and 400g of spinach, stirring until wilted.

In a separate bowl, combine 250g of mascarpone and 1 teaspoon of ground nutmeg. Then layer the lasagne sheets in an ovenproof dish, alternating with spoonfuls of the spinach and mascarpone mixture, plus 100 millilitres of double cream. Sprinkle over 100 grams of grated parmesan or a suitable vegetarian alternative.

Bake in the oven for 25 minutes until golden and bubbling. Serve with a side salad and enjoy! You can also freeze any leftovers, making this healthy spinach and mascarpone lasagne perfect for busy weeknights. Enjoy!

Spaghetti Alla Putanesca

Ingredients

400 grams of spaghetti
100 grams of pitted olives
1 tablespoon salted capers
500 grams of well-ripened tomatoes
or 400 grams of tomatoes in broth
2 large garlic cloves
5-6 anchovy fillets salted or in oil
1 sprig parsley
3-4 tablespoons olive oil
salt and pepper
optional: chilli pepper, fresh or dried

If you're looking for delicious recipes for kids, look no further than spaghetti alla Puttanesca. This classic Italian dish is easy to make and packed with flavour. Here's how to cook it:

Firstly, bring a large pot of salted water to a rolling boil and add the 400 grams of spaghetti. Cook until al dente, then strain and set aside.

In a large skillet over medium heat, add the 3-4 tablespoons of olive oil and two large cloves of garlic, chopped. When the garlic begins to sizzle, stir for about 30 seconds before adding anchovy fillets salted or in oil. Stir until the anchovies have dissolved into the oil.

Now you can add the pitted olives and capers, stirring for another 1-2 minutes before adding 500 grams of well-ripened tomatoes or 400 grams of tomatoes in broth. Season with salt and pepper to taste, plus chilli pepper if desired. Simmer for about 10 minutes until all the flavours have combined.

Finally, add the strained spaghetti and stir for 1-2 minutes to ensure everything is well mixed together. Serve in bowls with freshly chopped parsley as a garnish. Enjoy!

Creamy Chicken Pasta

Ingredients
500 g | 1lb large chicken breasts (or skinless boneless thighs)
Salt and pepper, to season.
1/2 tbsp olive oil, to fry the chicken.
1 tbsp unsalted butter.
3 garlic cloves, minced.
500 ml | 2 cups double / heavy cream (or you can use single cream)
50 g | ½ cup freshly grated Parmesan cheese.
1 tsp salt.

For delicious recipes for kids, try this Creamy Chicken Pasta! It's easy to make and takes less than 30 minutes. Start by seasoning the chicken breasts with salt and pepper. Heat oil in a large skillet over medium-high heat, then add the chicken breast. Cook until it turns golden brown on both sides, about 4 minutes per side. Once cooked, remove the chicken and set aside. In the same pan, melt butter over medium heat and add minced garlic. Cook for 1 minute until fragrant. Pour in the cream and bring it to a simmer before adding Parmesan cheese and salt. Stir everything together until combined, then add the cooked chicken back in the pan. Reduce heat to low and simmer for 10 minutes, stirring occasionally. Serve over cooked pasta of your choice and enjoy! With this delicious recipe, you can easily delight even the pickiest of eaters. Bon appetite!

Mushroom & Sausage Pasta

Ingredients

4 sausages, skin removed and meat squeezed out.
4 bacon rashers, diced.
200g mushrooms, chopped.
350g pasta shapes.
50g parmesan, grated, plus extra shavings to serve.
2 egg yolks.
small bunch parsley, finely chopped.
2 tbsp half-fat crème fraîche.

This delicious Mushroom & Sausage Pasta is the perfect meal for kids! It is packed with flavor from sausages, bacon, mushrooms, Parmesan and parsley. Plus it's so easy to make - all you need to do is follow these simple steps:

1. Start by removing the skin from the sausages and squeezing the meat out into a pan. Add the diced bacon and the mushrooms, then cook until the sausage and bacon are browned.

2. In a separate pan, bring some salted water to the boil and add your pasta shapes - these will need to be cooked for approximately 10 minutes until they are al dente.

3. While the pasta is cooking, add the egg yolks, parmesan and parsley to the sausage mixture and mix everything together.

4. When the pasta is cooked, drain it and then add it to the pan with the sausage mixture. Stir in the crème fraîche until everything is combined.

5. Serve the delicious Mushroom & Sausage Pasta with some extra parmesan shavings if you like. Enjoy!

With this delicious recipe, kids will love making and eating this delicious meal. Plus, it's so easy to make - no matter what level of cooking experience you have, anyone can whip up this delicious Mushroom & Sausage Pasta in no time! Enjoy!

Easy Scallop Pasta

Ingredients
6 scallops with corals.
6 slices prosciutto, halved lengthways.
175g fresh egg fettuccine or tagliatelle.
3 tbsp extra virgin olive oil, plus extra for drizzling (optional)
4 garlic cloves, finely chopped.
¼ tsp thyme leaf.
zest of 1 lemon and juice ½
4 tbsp dry white vermouth

This delicious scallop pasta dish is perfect for kids and adults alike! It's easy to make and requires just a few ingredients. Here's how you can cook it:

1. Preheat your oven to 200°C. Place the scallops on a baking tray lined with parchment paper, season with salt and pepper, and wrap each with a half slice of prosciutto. Bake for 8 minutes or until the scallops are cooked through and the prosciutto is crispy.

2. Meanwhile, cook the fresh egg fettuccine or tagliatelle in a large pan of salted boiling water according to packet instructions, then drain.

3. Heat the olive oil in a large non-stick frying pan over a medium heat, then add the garlic and thyme leaf. Cook for 1-2 minutes until fragrant before adding the cooked pasta, lemon zest and juice, and vermouth. Stir well to combine, then cook for a further 2 minutes.

4. Divide the pasta between plates and top with the cooked scallops. Drizzle over a little extra olive oil, if desired, before serving.

Enjoy this delicious scallop pasta dish for dinner tonight - it's sure to be a hit with your family! With its delicious flavor and easy-to-follow instructions, this is one of the best delicious recipes for kids out there. Perfect for a weeknight meal or fancy dinner party, you can't go wrong with this delicious dish. Bon appetit!

Easy Pesto Lasagne

Ingredients

190g jar pesto
500g tub mascarpone
200g bag spinach, roughly chopped
250g frozen pea
small pack basil, leaves chopped, and a few leaves reserved to finish
small pack mint, leaves chopped
12 fresh lasagne sheets
splash of milk
85g parmesan, grated (or vegetarian alternative)
50g pine nuts
green salad, to serve (optional)

This delicious pesto lasagne is an easy way to please even the pickiest eaters! Perfect for a weeknight dinner, this recipe is simple to make and full of delicious flavors. To begin, preheat your oven to 200 degrees Celsius (400 degrees Fahrenheit).

In a large bowl, stir together the jar of pesto, the mascarpone, chopped spinach, frozen peas, chopped basil, and chopped mint. Once combined, set aside.

In a large ovenproof dish, spread a layer of the pesto mixture on the bottom. Top with 3 lasagne sheets. Spread another layer of the pesto mixture over the top and sprinkle with parmesan or vegetarian alternative. Sprinkle with pine nuts and top with 3 more lasagne sheets.

Continue layering up the dish in this way, finishing with a layer of pesto mixture and parmesan. Pour over a splash of milk and sprinkle over some extra chopped basil leaves. Bake in the preheated oven for 25 minutes, until golden and bubbling.

This delicious pesto lasagne is a great recipe for kids to try their hand at cooking - sure to be a hit with the whole family! Serve warm with a green salad, if desired. Enjoy!

Tagliatelle With Vegetable Ragu

Are you looking for delicious recipes that your kids will love? Look no further than tagliatelle with vegetable ragu! This delicious Italian-inspired dish is quick and easy to cook, making it perfect for busy parents. With just a few simple ingredients, you can create a delicious dinner in no time.

To make the delicious tagliatelle with vegetable ragu, you'll need: 1 onion, finely chopped; 2 celery sticks, finely chopped; 2 carrots, diced; 4 garlic cloves, crushed; 1 tbsp each of tomato purée and balsamic vinegar; 250g diced vegetables such as courgettes, peppers and mushrooms; 50g red lentil; 2 x 400g cans of chopped tomatoes with basil; 250g tagliatelle (or your favourite pasta); 2 tbsp shaved parmesan (optional).

To begin, heat some oil in a large pan on a medium-high heat and add the onion, celery, carrots and garlic. Stir occasionally until softened, about 5 minutes.

Add the tomato purée and balsamic vinegar, stirring until evenly combined. Cook for a further 5 minutes.

Next, add the diced vegetables and red lentil to the pan and cook for around 10 minutes or until softened. Finally, add the canned tomatoes with basil, reduce the heat to low and simmer for 15-20 minutes.

Once the sauce is cooked, cook the tagliatelle according to the packet instructions. Once both are ready, you can serve with some freshly shaved parmesan if desired. Bon appetit!

Enjoy delicious meals made by your own hands with this delicious tagliatelle with vegetable ragu recipe! It's quick and easy to make, so it's perfect for busy parents who want delicious recipes their kids will love. Give it a try today!
Happy cooking! :)

Shrimps Alfredo Pasta

Shrimp Alfredo pasta is a delicious and easy recipe to make for kids. It's quick, delicious, and full of flavor! To start, you'll need to gather all the necessary ingredients: Fettuccine pasta, shrimp (I used frozen raw 31-40 count per pound size shrimp; you can use smaller or larger), butter (unsalted), cream cheese (for added texture and tangy taste), heavy cream, chicken broth (for added flavor), garlic, and Parmesan cheese.

Once you have all of the ingredients ready to go, start by cooking the fettuccine pasta according to package instructions. Once cooked, drain and set aside. In a large skillet or pan, heat butter over medium-high heat. Add the shrimp to the skillet and cook for 3-5 minutes or until they turn pink. Next, add in the garlic and sauté for 2 minutes. Add in cream cheese, heavy cream, and chicken broth and mix everything together until well combined. Lastly, add in the cooked fettuccine pasta and stir for 1-2 minutes until everything is well incorporated. Serve the delicious Shrimp Alfredo pasta with a generous helping of freshly grated Parmesan cheese. Enjoy!

This delicious Shrimp Alfredo pasta recipe is sure to please the whole family, kids included! It's an easy and delicious way to show your family how much you care. Plus, it's a great way to teach kids how to cook delicious recipes for themselves. So what are you waiting for? Give this delicious Shrimp Alfredo pasta recipe a try today!

Seafood Pasta

Ingredients

1 lb (454 g) scallops, fresh or thawed.
Kosher salt.
12 oz (340 g) good quality pasta.
3 Tbsp extra virgin olive oil.
8 large or 12 medium raw shrimp, fresh or frozen (and thawed) peeled, and deveined.
3 or 4 cloves minced garlic.
chopped Italian, flat leaf parsley.
freshly ground black pepper.

Seafood pasta is a delicious and easy-to-make meal that kids of all ages can enjoy. To prepare this delicious dish, start by bringing a pot of salted water to a boil before adding the pasta. Cook it until just al dente, then drain it and set aside.

In a large skillet over medium heat, heat the olive oil and garlic until fragrant. Add the scallops and shrimp, season with salt and pepper, and cook for 3-4 minutes or until cooked through. Add the cooked pasta to the skillet along with fresh parsley, and stir to combine everything together.

Serve your delicious seafood pasta in individual bowls accompanied by a side salad and delicious garlic bread. It's a delicious meal that kids are sure to love, and it's a great way to introduce them to the joys of cooking! Enjoy!

Cheesy Tortellini

Ingredients

2 cups cheese tortellini (fresh or frozen)
2 tablespoons salted butter.
2 cloves freshly minced garlic.
¼ teaspoon Italian seasoning.
¼ teaspoon salt.
freshly cracked pepper.
½ cup heavy cream.
2 tablespoons freshly grated Parmesan cheese.

Cheesy tortellini is a healthy and delicious pasta dish that can be prepared in just minutes. To make it, start by cooking the cheese tortellini according to the instructions on the package. Once cooked, set aside and melt butter in a large skillet over medium-high heat. Add garlic, Italian seasoning, salt, and pepper and sauté for 1-2 minutes until fragrant. Add the heavy cream to the skillet and bring to a simmer. Lastly, add the cooked tortellini and Parmesan cheese to the skillet and gently stir everything together until combined. Serve warm with extra Parmesan cheese on top if desired! Enjoy!

This cheesy tortellini dish is an easy yet healthy meal that the whole family will love. Make it for a weeknight dinner or a special occasion - either way, you're sure to have a winning dish on your hands! Enjoy!

Roasted Vegetables Pasta

This healthy roasted vegetable pasta dish is the perfect weeknight meal. The mix of vibrant vegetables and earthy flavors will keep your taste buds satisfied! For this recipe, you'll need 4 carrots, 2 Vidalia onions (or 1 small yellow onion), 5 small pattypan squash, 2 small zucchini, 10 cherry tomatoes, extra-virgin olive oil, sherry vinegar, and minced garlic.

To prepare the dish, preheat your oven to 425 degrees Fahrenheit. Place all of the vegetables on a large baking sheet and lightly drizzle with extra-virgin olive oil and season with salt and pepper. Roast for 25 minutes or until the veggies are soft and lightly browned.

In a large skillet, heat 1 tablespoon of olive oil over medium-high heat. Add the minced garlic and cook until fragrant (about 30 seconds). Add in the roasted vegetables, sherry vinegar, and cooked pasta. Toss to combine and season with salt and pepper to taste. Serve hot with an extra drizzle of olive oil. Enjoy!

Mushroom Pasta With Parmesan

Ingredients
8 ounces* short pasta, like penne, rigatoni, or casarecce, plus saved pasta water.
16 ounces baby bella (cremini) mushrooms (or a mix of other types)
1/2 small sweet onion or yellow onion.
4 tablespoons olive oil, divided.
¾ teaspoon kosher salt, divided.
3 tablespoons salted butter, divided.

This healthy mushroom pasta with parmesan is a quick and easy meal that can be made in 30 minutes or less! To prepare this dish, begin by boiling the 8 ounces of short pasta until al dente. Reserve some of the pasta water to use later when making your sauce. While the pasta cooks, heat 2 tablespoons of olive oil in a large skillet. Add in the mushrooms and onion, and season with 1/2 teaspoon of salt. Cook until the vegetables are softened and lightly browned, about 8-10 minutes. Remove from heat and set aside.

In a separate pan, melt 2 tablespoons of butter over medium heat. Once melted, add in the remaining 2 tablespoons of olive oil, and the cooked vegetables. Give everything a good stir to combine. Continue cooking for another 5 minutes or so until the sauce is golden and bubbly. Add in the reserved pasta water, 1/4 teaspoon of kosher salt, and freshly grated parmesan cheese (to taste). Stir to combine, then add in the cooked pasta. Give everything a good stir before serving! Enjoy your healthy mushroom pasta with parmesan hot, topped with extra parmesan cheese and freshly chopped parsley if desired. Bon Appétit!

Avocado Fusilli Pasta

Ingredients

350g fusilli.
2 cloves garlic, peeled.
200g baby spinach.
2 small ripe avocados, halved and stoned.
extra-virgin olive oil, for drizzling.
30g roasted cashews, chopped.
30g roasted almonds, chopped.
a small bunch coriander, chopped.

For healthy and delicious pasta, you can't go wrong with this avocado fusilli recipe! Start by bringing a large pot of salted water to the boil. Add the fusilli and cook until al dente. Meanwhile, in a large pan over medium heat, add some olive oil and garlic cloves. Saute for 5 minutes until fragrant. Add the baby spinach and cook for a few minutes until wilted. When the pasta is cooked, drain it and add to the pan with the spinach mixture. Finally, top with halved avocados, roasted cashews and almonds and chopped coriander. Drizzle with some extra-virgin olive oil for a healthy finish. Serve and enjoy! This healthy pasta dish is sure to become a favorite in your house. With its creamy avocado, crunchy nuts, and delicious flavors from the garlic, spinach and coriander, it's an easy healthy meal that everyone can enjoy. Try this avocado fusilli recipe today!

Baked Rigatoni Pasta

Ingredients

1 pound rigatoni.
1 pound ground Italian sausage.
1 pound 90/10 ground beef.
1 cup diced yellow onion.
4 garlic cloves, minced.
1 (24 ounce) jar marinara sauce or homemade.
1 (24 ounce) can crushed tomatoes.
1 teaspoon kosher salt.

If you're looking for a healthy and hearty pasta dish, look no further than baked rigatoni! This delicious meal is loaded with healthy ingredients like Italian sausage, ground beef, diced onion, garlic and marinara sauce. Plus it comes together in just one pot for easy preparation. Here's how to make this tasty dish:

Begin by preheating the oven to 350°F. Then, bring a large pot of salted water to a boil and add 1 pound of rigatoni. Cook for 8-10 minutes, stirring occasionally until al dente. Drain and set aside.

In a large skillet over medium-high heat, brown the Italian sausage and ground beef until fully cooked, stirring occasionally. Add the diced yellow onion and minced garlic and sauté until softened, about 3-4 minutes.

Transfer the meat mixture to a large baking dish, then add in the marinara sauce/homemade sauce, crushed tomatoes and salt. Stir everything together. Add the drained rigatoni and stir everything together to evenly coat in the sauce.

Cover the dish with aluminum foil and bake for 20 minutes or until bubbling. Remove from oven and let cool for a few minutes before serving. Enjoy!

Roasted Eggplant Pasta

Ingredients
1 large eggplant, cut into cubes.
1 small yellow onion, chopped (or half of a large onion)
1-2 Tablespoons oil.
1/2 teaspoon garlic powder.
2-3 cups tomato sauce.
1 16 oz. box of pasta noodles (see notes)
salt & black peppers.
fresh basil *optional.

This healthy roasted eggplant pasta dish is the perfect way to enjoy a cozy meal on any night of the week. Using just a few simple ingredients, this Italian-inspired dish comes together quickly and easily for an impressive dinner that's sure to please.

To begin, preheat your oven to 400 degrees Fahrenheit. Place the cubed eggplant on a baking sheet and drizzle it with oil. Sprinkle the garlic powder and salt & pepper over top, then give the eggplant cubes a good stir to evenly coat them with the seasonings. Roast in the oven for 30-35 minutes until lightly browned and tender.

Meanwhile, prepare your pasta noodles according to the package instructions. When cooked, drain and set aside.

In a large skillet or Dutch oven, heat the remaining oil over medium-high heat. Add in the chopped onion and cook for 5 minutes or until softened. Add in the tomato sauce and stir to combine. Once bubbling, reduce heat to low and simmer for 10 minutes.

Add the roasted eggplant and cooked pasta noodles to the sauce and stir to combine. Simmer everything together for 3-5 minutes, then remove from heat. Serve with a sprinkle of fresh basil, if desired. Enjoy!

Pomodoro Sauce

Ingredients

5 pounds peeled fresh tomatoes or 3 28-ounce cans of San Marzano whole peeled tomatoes.
2 tablespoons olive oil.
½ peeled and finely minced/grated yellow onion.
4 finely minced/grated garlic cloves.
12-15 fresh basil leaves.
sea salt and pepper to taste.
cooked pasta.

Pomodoro pasta is a healthy and delicious dish to make at home. It's simple to prepare and requires just a few fresh ingredients.

To begin, heat the olive oil in a large saucepan over high heat. Once it's hot, add the onion and garlic, cooking until fragrant - about three minutes. Then, add the tomatoes and all seasonings. Simmer for 15-20 minutes, stirring occasionally to prevent burning. Once the sauce is thickened and reduced, reduce the heat and add the fresh basil leaves.

Meanwhile, cook your pasta according to package instructions until al dente (it will finish cooking in the sauce). Drain in and add to the pomodoro sauce, stirring until everything is well combined. Season with more salt and pepper if desired.

Enjoy your healthy home-cooked pomodoro pasta! Serve it alone or topped with freshly grated Parmesan cheese. Enjoy!

Cherry Tomato Pasta

Ingredients

12 ounces bucatini pasta.
⅓ cup extra-virgin olive oil, more for drizzling.
3 garlic cloves, sliced.
3 pints cherry tomatoes, divided.
2½ tablespoons capers.
2 teaspoons lemon zest.
1 teaspoon balsamic vinegar.
1 teaspoon sea salt.

This healthy bucatini pasta dish is sure to please any pasta lover! To prepare it, start by cooking the bucatini in a large pot of salted boiling water until al dente.

Meanwhile, heat ⅓ cup of extra-virgin olive oil in a large skillet over medium heat and add the garlic slices. Cook until the garlic begins to turn golden, then add half of the cherry tomatoes and the capers. Cook for 3-4 minutes, stirring often, until all ingredients are well combined.

Once the bucatini is done cooking, drain it and add it to the skillet with the tomato mixture. Add the remaining cherry tomatoes, lemon zest, balsamic vinegar, and sea salt. Stir to combine all ingredients and cook for an additional 2-3 minutes.

Serve the healthy bucatini pasta while warm, drizzled with extra-virgin olive oil if desired. Enjoy!

Lemon Pasta

Ingredients

8 oz. package pasta (any long noodle)
2 - 3 tablespoons vegan butter or olive oil.
3 garlic cloves, minced.
1/4 teaspoon red pepper flakes, or to taste.
2 - 3 lemons (about 1/4 - 1/2 cup), juice of and some zest.
1/4 cup parsley, chopped.
salt & pepper, to taste.

If you're looking for a healthy and delicious pasta dish, this vegan Lemon Pasta is the perfect recipe for you. It's quick and easy to prepare, using simple ingredients like vegan butter or olive oil, minced garlic, red pepper flakes, lemons (juice of and zest), parsley, salt & pepper.

This dish is healthy, flavorful, and sure to impress!

To begin, cook the pasta according to the package instructions. Meanwhile, heat a large skillet over medium heat. Add in vegan butter or olive oil, garlic and red pepper flakes. Cook until fragrant and the garlic has softened slightly (about 1 minute). Stir in the lemon juice and zest and cook for an additional minute.

Drain the cooked pasta and add it to the skillet. Add in parsley, salt & pepper to taste, stirring until combined. Serve the lemon pasta warm with extra red pepper flakes, if desired. Enjoy!

Pasta With Salmon And Peas

Looking for delicious recipes that are perfect for kids? This delicious pasta dish with salmon and peas is a great option. Not only is it easy to make, but it's packed full of flavour and packed full of protein and other essential nutrients. To make this delicious recipe, you will need the following ingredients: 240g wholewheat fusilli, a knob of butter, 1 large shallot finely chopped, 140g frozen peas, 2 skinless salmon fillets cut into chunks, 140g low-fat crème fraîche, ½ low-salt vegetable stock cube and a small bunch of chives snipped.

To begin, heat the butter in a large pan over a medium heat. Once melted, add the shallot and cook until softened for about 3 minutes. Then add the peas and salmon chunks, cook for 2 minutes, stirring constantly. Add the crème fraîche and stock cube to the pan and stir everything together until combined. Finally, add the fusilli to the pan and mix everything together. Cook for 8-10 minutes, stirring often.

Once the fusilli is cooked and all of the ingredients are combined, sprinkle over the chives and serve. Your delicious pasta dish with salmon and peas is now ready to be enjoyed by your family! Enjoy!

Sage Lasagna

9 to 12 lasagna noodles (6 to 8 ounces, gluten-free if necessary)
1 ½ tablespoons chopped fresh sage, divided, plus additional leaves as desired
Zest of 1/2 lemon (about 2 teaspoons)
⅛ teaspoon ground nutmeg
½ cup plus 2 tablespoons milk
16 ounces (2 cups) whole milk ricotta cheese
¼ teaspoon kosher salt

When it comes to healthy pasta dishes, lasagna sage is a great option. Preparing the dish starts with boiling 9 to 12 lasagna noodles - 6 to 8 ounces, gluten-free if necessary - until they are al dente. In the meantime, in a bowl combine 1 ½ tablespoons chopped fresh sage, the zest of half a lemon (about 2 teaspoons), ⅛ teaspoon ground nutmeg, ½ cup plus 2 tablespoons milk, 16 ounces (2 cups) whole milk ricotta cheese and ¼ teaspoon kosher salt. Once the noodles are cooked and drained, spread a layer of the ricotta mixture over them. Then top with additional sage leaves as desired. Cover with foil and bake in a preheated 375°F oven for 45 minutes. Enjoy your delicious healthy lasagna sage!

Bacon Mushroom Pasta

Ingredients

8 ounces uncooked pasta (I used bucatini)
6 strips bacon cut into small pieces.
7 ounces cremini mushrooms sliced.
2 cloves garlic minced.
1/3 cup chicken broth or dry white wine.
1/4 teaspoon Italian seasoning.
1 teaspoon lemon juice.
1 teaspoon flour.

If you're looking for delicious recipes that kids will love, this bacon mushroom pasta is the perfect choice. It's easy to make and packed with flavor. To start, cook 8 ounces of uncooked bucatini pasta according to package instructions. Once cooked, drain and set aside.

In a large skillet over medium-high heat, cook the bacon until crisp, about 5 minutes. Remove the bacon with a slotted spoon and set aside. To the same skillet, add 7 ounces of sliced cremini mushrooms and cook for 4-5 minutes or until softened.

Add 2 cloves of minced garlic to the skillet and sauté for an additional 30 seconds. Add in 1/3 cup of chicken broth or dry white wine and simmer for 2 minutes. Stir in 1/4 teaspoon of Italian seasoning, 1 teaspoon of lemon juice, and 1 teaspoon of flour.

Return the bacon to the skillet and add the cooked pasta. Continue cooking until the sauce has thickened, stirring occasionally. Serve hot with freshly grated Parmesan cheese.

This delicious bacon mushroom pasta is sure to be a hit with the kids, and it's simple enough for even beginner cooks to prepare. With a few simple ingredients and easy-to-follow instructions, you can have this delicious dish on the table in no time! Give this delicious recipe a try tonight! Enjoy

Pasta Bolognese

Ingredients

1 tbsp olive oil.
4 rashers smoked streaky bacon, finely chopped.
2 medium onions, finely chopped.
2 carrots, trimmed and finely chopped.
2 celery sticks, finely chopped.
2 garlic cloves finely chopped.
2-3 sprigs rosemary leaves picked and finely chopped.
500g beef mince.

Pasta bolognese is one of those delicious recipes that kids will love. And it's a great way to introduce them to cooking at home. Here's how to make it:
Start by heating the olive oil in a large saucepan over medium heat. Add the bacon, onions, carrots and celery sticks and cook, stirring regularly, for about 5 minutes. Next, add the garlic and rosemary leaves and cook for a further 2 minutes.

Add the mince to the pan, breaking it up with a wooden spoon as it cooks. Cook until browned all over, then reduce heat and simmer for 10-15 minutes.
Finally, add the tomato puree and season to taste. Cook for a further 10 minutes or until thickened then serve with your favorite pasta. Enjoy!
This delicious pasta bolognese dish is sure to be loved by kids and adults alike. With just a few simple ingredients, it's easy to make and can be on the dinner table in just under 30 minutes. So the next time you need a delicious and family-friendly meal, try out this delicious pasta bolognese!

Bon Appetite!

Vegetarian Lasagna

Vegetarian lasagna makes a delicious, kid-friendly meal. It's easy to make and packed with nutrition from vegetables like carrots, bell peppers, zucchini, and onion. To get started on this delicious recipe, you'll need the following ingredients: 2 tablespoons extra-virgin olive oil, 3 large carrots (chopped into about 1 cup), 1 red bell pepper (chopped), 1 medium zucchini (chopped), 1 medium yellow onion (chopped), ¼ teaspoon salt, and 5 to 6 ounces of baby spinach.

To begin cooking your vegetarian lasagna, heat the olive oil in a skillet over medium-high heat. Add the carrots, bell pepper, zucchini, onion, and salt. Cook the vegetables until they are soft and tender, stirring occasionally. Then, add the spinach and cook for a few minutes longer until it wilts.

Once your vegetables are cooked through, you are ready to assemble your delicious vegetarian lasagna! Layer a baking dish with pre-cooked lasagna noodles, followed by the cooked vegetable mixture and then some delicious sauce. Top with shredded cheese and bake in an oven preheated to 350 degrees for 30 minutes. Your delicious vegetarian lasagna is now ready to enjoy - a perfect meal that kids will love!

Making vegetarian meals doesn't have to be difficult. With delicious recipes like this vegetarian lasagna, you can easily create delicious and nutritious meals that the whole family will enjoy. Give it a try today!

Fettuccine Alfredo

Ingredients

227g tub clotted cream.
25g butter (about 2 tbsp)
1 tsp cornflour.
100g parmesan, grated.
freshly grated nutmeg.
250g fresh fettuccine or tagliatelle.
snipped chives or chopped parsley, to serve (optional)
!

Fettuccine Alfredo is a delicious and easy-to-make recipe for kids. It's the perfect dish for family dinners or impressing your friends! Here's how to make it:

1. Start by bringing a large pot of salted water to a boil over medium-high heat.

2. Once the water is boiling, add the fresh fettuccine or tagliatelle and cook for about 8-10 minutes until it's al dente.

3. While the pasta cooks, prepare the sauce: In a separate pan, melt the butter over medium-high heat before adding in the clotted cream. Once combined, add in the cornflour, grated parmesan cheese, and a pinch of nutmeg. Stir until everything is combined.

4. Once the pasta is cooked, drain it and add it to the sauce pan with the sauce ingredients. Stir until the pasta is evenly coated before serving with snipped chives or chopped parsley (optional).

Fettuccine Alfredo is a delicious, easy-to-make recipe for kids and adults alike. Enjoy this delicious dish with family or friends - bon appetit!

Ravioli Lasagna

This delicious ravioli lasagna recipe is sure to be a hit with kids and adults alike! To make this delicious dish, you will need 1 pound of ground beef, 1 jar (28 ounces) spaghetti sauce, 1 package (25 ounces) frozen sausage or cheese ravioli, 1-1/2 cups shredded part-skim mozzarella cheese and minced fresh basil (optional).

Begin by cooking the ground beef in a large skillet over medium-high heat until no longer pink, stirring occasionally. Drain off any fat. Add spaghetti sauce to the cooked beef and bring mixture to a boil. Reduce heat; simmer for about 10 minutes or until heated through, stirring occasionally.

Meanwhile, cook ravioli according to package directions. Drain and set aside. Preheat oven to 350°F (175°C). In a greased 13x9-inch baking dish, layer one-third of the beef mixture, half of the cooked ravioli, and one-third of the cheese. Repeat layers. Top with remaining beef mixture and cheese.

Bake, uncovered, for 25 to 30 minutes or until bubbly and cheese is melted. If desired, sprinkle with basil before serving. Enjoy! With a few simple ingredients, this delicious recipe makes an easy meal that the whole family will love! Try it today for a delicious meal that will keep the kids asking for more. Bon Appétit!

Pesto Pasta

Ingredients

6 ounces spaghetti, reserve 1/2 cup starchy pasta water.
1/3 to 1/2 cup. basil pesto or vegan pesto.
Extra-virgin olive oil, for drizzling.
Fresh lemon juice, as desired.
4 cups arugula.
2 tablespoons pine nuts.
Pinches of red pepper flakes.
Sea salt and freshly ground black pepper.

Cooking delicious recipes for kids doesn't have to be complicated. With the right ingredients, you can make delicious pesto pasta in a flash! To begin, bring a large pot of salted water to a boil and add the spaghetti. Cook according to package instructions until al dente. Reserve 1/2 cup of starchy pasta water before straining.

In a large bowl, mix together the basil pesto, arugula and pine nuts and season with salt, pepper and red pepper flakes to taste. Next, add the cooked spaghetti to the pesto mixture along with a little of the reserved pasta water to thin out the sauce if desired. Drizzle with extra-virgin olive oil and lemon juice, if desired.

Give the delicious pesto pasta a good stir to coat all the ingredients evenly. Plate up and enjoy! This delicious recipe is sure to be a hit with kids of all ages and tastes great as leftovers too. Give it a try today and enjoy some delicious pesto pasta for dinner tonight!

Happy cooking!

Creamy Salmon Pasta

Ingredients
2 salmon fillets.
1 tbsp olive oil, plus 1 tsp if roasting.
175g penne.
2 shallots or 1 small onion, finely chopped.
1 garlic clove, crushed.
100ml white wine.
200ml double cream or crème fraîche.
¼ lemon, zested and juiced.

Creamy salmon pasta is a delicious and easy recipe for kids. This delicious meal can be prepared in just a few simple steps.

To begin, preheat your oven to 200°c (gas mark 6) and brush the salmon fillets with 1 tbsp of olive oil. Place them in the oven to bake for 12-15 minutes until cooked through. Once the salmon is cooked, flake it into small pieces and set aside.

Bring a large pot of salted water to the boil and cook your penne according to packet instructions until al dente.

Meanwhile, heat 1 tsp of olive oil in a large skillet over medium-high heat. Add the shallots or onions and garlic to the skillet and sauté for a few minutes until softened. Add the white wine, cream or crème fraîche, lemon zest, lemon juice and flaked salmon pieces. Simmer gently over low heat for around 5-7 minutes until the sauce has thickened slightly.

To serve, drain the cooked penne and combine with the sauce. Divide into plates and enjoy your delicious creamy salmon pasta!

This delicious recipe is sure to be a hit with all the family - even picky eaters will love it! With only a few simple ingredients, this meal can be prepared in no time at all so why not give it a try tonight? Enjoy!

Meatballs Spaghetti

Meatball spaghetti is a delicious and easy-to-make recipe for kids. This delicious dish is made with spaghetti noodles, ground beef, bread crumbs, parsley, Parmesan cheese, egg, garlic cloves, salt, red pepper flakes, extra-virgin olive oil, onion chopped finely, crushed tomatoes and one bay leaf.

To begin, cook the spaghetti noodles according to package instructions. While the pasta is cooking, prepare the meatballs: In a large bowl combine ground beef, bread crumbs, parsley, Parmesan cheese, egg and garlic cloves. Using your hands or a wooden spoon mix until everything is combined. Form into small balls about 1 inch in diameter, and set aside.

Heat a large skillet over medium heat and add the olive oil. Add the meatballs to the pan and cook until golden brown all over, about 5 minutes. Remove from the heat and set aside.

Add the onion to the same skillet over medium-high heat and sauté for 3 minutes. Add the crushed tomatoes, bay leaf and red pepper flakes and season with salt and pepper to taste. Bring to a simmer and add the cooked meatballs back into the sauce. Simmer for about 10 minutes until sauce has thickened.

Once spaghetti is done cooking, drain it and toss it in the skillet with the meatballs and sauce. Mix everything together and serve with freshly grated Parmesan cheese on top. Enjoy!

Meatball spaghetti is a delicious dish that can be enjoyed by the whole family. With its delicious combination of ingredients, it's sure to be a hit in any household! Try this delicious recipe today and enjoy delicious Italian-style food with your family and friends. Buon Appetito!

Carbonara Spaghetti

Carbonara spaghetti is a delicious recipe for kids to learn how to cook. The ingredients you will need are 100g of pancetta, 50g of pecorino cheese, 50g of parmesan, 3 large eggs, 350g of spaghetti, 2 plump garlic cloves (peeled and left whole), 50g unsalted butter, sea salt, and freshly ground black pepper. To begin cooking this delicious dish, bring a large saucepan of salted water to the boil. Add the spaghetti and cook until al dente (around 8-10 minutes). Meanwhile, fry the pancetta in a dry non-stick frying pan over moderate heat for about 5 minutes until lightly golden. Once cooked, set aside and keep warm. In a small bowl, mix together the pecorino cheese and parmesan with the eggs until you have a creamy sauce. Season well with salt and pepper. When the spaghetti is cooked, drain it, reserving some of the cooking water. Add the spaghetti to the pan with the pancetta and garlic, and stir everything together. Add the butter, stirring until melted. Pour over the egg mixture and toss everything together well with a little of the reserved cooking water - this will help to make it nice and creamy. Serve immediately while still warm. Enjoy!

This delicious carbonara spaghetti dish is sure to be a hit with the whole family. With just a few ingredients and simple steps, your kids can learn to make this delicious dinner in no time! Serve it with a fresh salad on the side for a delicious meal that everyone will love. Enjoy!

Tuna Pasta

Ingredients

2 tablespoons olive oil.
2 large cloves garlic minced.
1 (5 ounce) can tuna, drained I prefer tuna packed in oil.
1 teaspoon lemon juice.
1 tablespoon fresh parsley chopped.
Salt & pepper to taste.
4 ounces uncooked pasta (I used spaghetti)

Tuna pasta is a delicious and easy-to-make recipe for kids. It's perfect for busy weeknights when you don't have much time to cook. To make this delicious dish, start by heating the olive oil in a large skillet over medium heat. Add the garlic and sauté until fragrant, about 1 minute. Add the tuna and stir to combine. Then add the lemon juice and parsley, season with salt and pepper to taste, and cook for another minute or two. Finally, add the uncooked pasta to the skillet and mix everything together. Cook according to directions on the box until al dente. Serve hot and enjoy! Tuna pasta is a delicious and nutritious meal that your kids will love. Enjoy!

Turkey Sausage with Pasta

Ingredients:

8 ounces of whole wheat pasta
1 tablespoon olive oil
1 small onion, diced
2 cloves garlic, minced
4 turkey sausages, casings removed
1 red bell pepper, diced
1 cup sliced mushrooms
1 cup marinara sauce
1 teaspoon dried oregano
1/2 teaspoon dried basil
Salt and pepper to taste
Fresh parsley, chopped (for garnish)

Instructions:

Cook the pasta according to the package instructions until al dente. Drain and set aside.
Heat the olive oil in a large skillet over medium heat. Add the diced onion and minced garlic, and sauté until fragrant and translucent.
Add the turkey sausages to the skillet, breaking them up with a spatula or wooden spoon. Cook until browned and cooked through.
Add the diced red bell pepper and sliced mushrooms to the skillet. Cook for an additional 3-4 minutes until the vegetables are tender.
Stir in the marinara sauce, dried oregano, dried basil, salt, and pepper. Reduce the heat to low and let the sauce simmer for about 5 minutes to allow the flavors to meld together.
Add the cooked pasta to the skillet and toss to coat it evenly with the sauce
Cook for another 2-3 minutes until the pasta is heated through.
Remove from heat and garnish with freshly chopped parsley.
Serve the turkey sausage with pasta warm and enjoy!

Chicken And Bacon Pasta

Ingredients needed
- boneless skinless chicken breast.
- smoked pancetta lardons (or bacon)
- chicken stock (made from a stock cube)
- parsley.
- garlic.
- onion.
- double cream.
- pasta shells.

Are you looking for delicious recipes that the whole family can enjoy? Look no further than this delicious chicken and bacon pasta! This delicious dish is perfect for picky eaters, and it's easy to make too. To get started, you'll need boneless skinless chicken breast, smoked pancetta lardons (or bacon), chicken stock (made from a stock cube), parsley, garlic, onion, double cream and some pasta shells.

Once you have all the ingredients ready to go, it's time to start cooking! Begin by heating up some butter or oil in a large saucepan over medium heat. Once the butter is melted, add the lardons and cook until golden. Add the garlic and onion to the pan, cooking for about 2 minutes until fragrant. Then add in the chicken breast and cook for 4-5 minutes, stirring occasionally.

Add the chicken stock to the pan and bring it to a gentle simmer before adding in the cream and parsley. Stir everything together and reduce the heat to low. Let the sauce simmer for about 10-15 minutes until it has reduced and thickened.

Add in your cooked pasta shells and stir them through the sauce. Serve hot with a parsley on top and enjoy! With this delicious chicken and bacon pasta recipe, you'll have a meal that kids and adults will love. Enjoy!

Buffalo Chicken Pasta

Ingredients:

8 ounces of penne pasta
2 boneless, skinless chicken breasts, cooked and shredded
1 tablespoon olive oil
1/4 cup unsalted butter
1/2 cup buffalo hot sauce
1/2 cup ranch dressing (vegan option available)
1/4 cup diced celery
1/4 cup diced carrots
1/4 cup diced bell peppers (any color)
1/2 teaspoon garlic powder
Salt and pepper to taste
Fresh parsley, chopped (for garnish)

Instructions:

Cook the penne pasta according to the package instructions until al dente. Drain and set aside.
In a large skillet, heat olive oil over medium heat. Add the diced celery, carrots, and bell peppers. Sauté for 3-4 minutes until the vegetables are slightly tender.
In the same skillet, add the cooked and shredded chicken breast. Stir in the buffalo hot sauce and garlic powder. Cook for an additional 2-3 minutes, allowing the flavors to meld together.
Reduce the heat to low and add the butter to the skillet. Stir until the butter is melted and incorporated into the sauce.
Stir in the ranch dressing and season with salt and pepper to taste. Simmer for 2-3 minutes to heat the sauce thoroughly.
Add the cooked penne pasta to the skillet and toss it with the buffalo chicken sauce until the pasta is evenly coated.
Cook for another 2-3 minutes to heat the pasta through.
Remove from heat and garnish with freshly chopped parsley.
Serve the buffalo chicken pasta warm and enjoy!
Note: Adjust the amount of buffalo hot sauce according to your child's spice preference. You can also add some steamed broccoli or peas to the dish for added nutrition and color.

Tender Beef over Noodles

Ingredients:

8 ounces egg noodles
1 tablespoon olive oil
1/2 pound beef sirloin, thinly sliced
1/2 teaspoon garlic powder
1/2 teaspoon onion powder
1/2 teaspoon paprika
Salt and pepper to taste
1 cup beef broth
1 tablespoon soy sauce (or tamari for gluten-free option)
1 tablespoon cornstarch (or arrowroot powder for gluten-free option)
1/2 cup frozen peas
1/2 cup sliced carrots
Fresh parsley, chopped (for garnish)

Instructions:

Cook the egg noodles according to the package instructions until al dente. Drain and set aside.
In a large skillet, heat olive oil over medium heat. Add the thinly sliced beef sirloin and season it with garlic powder, onion powder, paprika, salt, and pepper. Cook until the beef is browned and cooked to your desired doneness. Remove the cooked beef from the skillet and set it aside.
In the same skillet, add the beef broth and soy sauce. Whisk in the cornstarch until it's fully dissolved in the liquid.
Add the frozen peas and sliced carrots to the skillet. Bring the mixture to a simmer and cook for about 5 minutes, or until the vegetables are tender.
Return the cooked beef to the skillet and stir it with the vegetables and sauce. Cook for an additional 2-3 minutes to heat everything through and allow the flavors to meld together.
Serve the tender beef mixture over the cooked egg noodles.
Garnish with freshly chopped parsley.
Serve the tender beef over noodles warm and enjoy!
Note: You can add other vegetables such as broccoli or bell peppers to the dish if your child enjoys them. Feel free to adjust the seasonings according to your child's taste preferences.

Chicken and Bows

Ingredients:

8 ounces bowtie pasta
2 boneless, skinless chicken breasts, cut into bite-sized pieces
1 tablespoon olive oil
1/2 teaspoon garlic powder
1/2 teaspoon dried oregano
1/2 teaspoon dried basil
1/2 cup chicken broth
1 cup frozen peas
1/2 cup diced carrots
1/2 cup diced bell peppers (any color)
Salt and pepper to taste
Fresh parsley, chopped (for garnish)

Instructions:

Cook the bowtie pasta according to the package instructions until al dente. Drain and set aside.
In a large skillet, heat olive oil over medium heat. Add the chicken pieces, garlic powder, dried oregano, dried basil, salt, and pepper. Cook until the chicken is browned and cooked through.
Remove the cooked chicken from the skillet and set it aside.
In the same skillet, add the chicken broth and bring it to a simmer. Add the frozen peas, diced carrots, and diced bell peppers. Cook for about 5 minutes or until the vegetables are tender.
Return the cooked chicken to the skillet and stir it with the vegetables.
Add the cooked bowtie pasta to the skillet and toss it with the chicken and vegetable mixture until well combined.
Cook for an additional 2-3 minutes to heat the pasta through.
Remove from heat and garnish with freshly chopped parsley.
Serve the chicken and bows warm and enjoy!
Note: You can customize this recipe by adding other vegetables that your child enjoys, such as broccoli or corn. Feel free to sprinkle some grated Parmesan cheese (vegan option available) on top for added flavor if desired.

Italian Sausage with Bow Ties

Ingredients:

8 ounces bowtie pasta
1 tablespoon olive oil
4 Italian sausage links (mild or spicy), casings removed
1 small onion, diced
2 cloves garlic, minced
1 cup marinara sauce
1 teaspoon dried basil
1/2 teaspoon dried oregano
Salt and pepper to taste
Fresh parsley, chopped (for garnish)
Grated Parmesan cheese (optional)

Instructions:

Cook the bowtie pasta according to the package instructions until al dente. Drain and set aside.
In a large skillet, heat the olive oil over medium heat. Add the diced onion and minced garlic, and sauté until fragrant and translucent.
Add the Italian sausage to the skillet, breaking it up with a spatula or wooden spoon. Cook until browned and cooked through.
Stir in the marinara sauce, dried basil, dried oregano, salt, and pepper. Reduce the heat to low and let the sauce simmer for about 5 minutes to allow the flavors to meld together.
Add the cooked bowtie pasta to the skillet and toss it with the sausage sauce until the pasta is evenly coated.
Cook for another 2-3 minutes to heat the pasta through.
Remove from heat and garnish with freshly chopped parsley.
Optionally, sprinkle some grated Parmesan cheese on top for added flavor.
Serve the Italian sausage with bow ties warm and enjoy!
Note: You can add diced bell peppers, sliced mushrooms, or any other vegetables your child enjoys to the skillet along with the onions and garlic. Customize the level of spiciness by choosing mild or spicy Italian sausage. If you prefer a vegan option, you can substitute the Italian sausage with plant-based sausage alternatives.

Tortellini Carbonara

Ingredients:

8 ounces tortellini (your choice of filling)
4 slices of bacon, chopped
1 tablespoon unsalted butter
2 cloves garlic, minced
2 large eggs
1/2 cup grated Parmesan cheese
Salt and pepper to taste
Fresh parsley, chopped (for garnish)

Instructions:

Cook the tortellini according to the package instructions until al dente. Drain and set aside.
In a large skillet, cook the chopped bacon over medium heat until crispy. Remove the bacon from the skillet and set it aside, leaving the bacon drippings in the pan.
In the same skillet, melt the butter in the bacon drippings over medium heat. Add the minced garlic and sauté until fragrant, about 1-2 minutes.
In a bowl, whisk together the eggs and grated Parmesan cheese until well combined.
Reduce the heat to low and add the cooked tortellini to the skillet with the garlic and butter. Stir to coat the tortellini with the mixture.
Pour the egg and cheese mixture over the tortellini in the skillet, stirring quickly to combine. The heat from the skillet will cook the eggs and create a creamy sauce. Make sure to stir continuously to prevent the eggs from scrambling.
Add the cooked bacon back to the skillet and toss it with the tortellini and sauce.
Season with salt and pepper to taste.
Remove from heat and garnish with freshly chopped parsley.
Serve the Tortellini Carbonara warm and enjoy!
Note: You can add vegetables such as peas, chopped spinach, or diced bell peppers to the dish for added nutrition and color. Feel free to customize the recipe by using different types of tortellini fillings, such as cheese, spinach, or mushroom.

Double Jack Mac

Ingredients:

8 ounces elbow macaroni
2 tablespoons unsalted butter
2 tablespoons all-purpose flour
2 cups milk (dairy or plant-based)
2 cups shredded cheddar cheese
1 cup shredded Monterey Jack cheese
1/2 teaspoon garlic powder
1/2 teaspoon onion powder
Salt and pepper to taste
Optional toppings: chopped green onions, diced tomatoes, cooked and crumbled bacon (or vegan bacon), or breadcrumbs

Instructions:

Cook the elbow macaroni according to the package instructions until al dente. Drain and set aside.
In a large saucepan, melt the butter over medium heat. Add the flour and whisk until well combined to form a roux.
Gradually pour in the milk while whisking constantly to prevent lumps from forming. Continue to whisk until the mixture thickens.
Add the shredded cheddar cheese and shredded Monterey Jack cheese to the saucepan, reserving a small amount of each for topping. Stir until the cheeses are melted and the sauce is smooth.
Stir in the garlic powder, onion powder, salt, and pepper to taste. Adjust the seasonings according to your child's preference.
Add the cooked elbow macaroni to the cheese sauce and stir until the pasta is well coated.
Optional: If desired, sprinkle the reserved shredded cheese, chopped green onions, diced tomatoes, cooked and crumbled bacon (or vegan bacon), or breadcrumbs on top.
Preheat the oven broiler on low heat. Place the saucepan under the broiler for a few minutes until the toppings are melted or lightly browned (if using).
Remove from the oven and let it cool slightly before serving.
Serve the Double Jack Mac warm and enjoy!
Note: You can customize this recipe by adding vegetables such as peas, broccoli, or diced bell peppers to the dish for added nutrition and color. Feel free to adjust the types and amounts of cheese based on your child's taste preferences.

Lasagna Casserole

Ingredients:

8 lasagna noodles
1 tablespoon olive oil
1 pound ground beef (or ground turkey or plant-based ground meat substitute)
1 small onion, diced
2 cloves garlic, minced
1 can (14.5 ounces) diced tomatoes
1 can (6 ounces) tomato paste
1 teaspoon dried basil
1 teaspoon dried oregano
1/2 teaspoon garlic powder
Salt and pepper to taste
2 cups shredded mozzarella cheese
Fresh parsley, chopped (for garnish)

Instructions:

Preheat the oven to 375°F (190°C).
Cook the lasagna noodles according to the package instructions until al dente. Drain and set aside.
In a large skillet, heat the olive oil over medium heat. Add the diced onion and minced garlic, and sauté until fragrant and translucent.
Add the ground beef to the skillet and cook until browned and cooked through. If using plant-based ground meat substitute, follow the package instructions for cooking.
Drain any excess grease from the skillet if necessary.
Add the diced tomatoes, tomato paste, dried basil, dried oregano, garlic powder, salt, and pepper to the skillet. Stir to combine all the ingredients and let the sauce simmer for about 5 minutes.
Grease a 9x13-inch baking dish.
Spread a thin layer of the meat sauce on the bottom of the baking dish.
Arrange a layer of cooked lasagna noodles over the sauce.
Spoon another layer of the meat sauce over the noodles.
Sprinkle a generous amount of shredded mozzarella cheese on top of the sauce.
Repeat steps 9-11, layering noodles, sauce, and cheese until you have used all the noodles and sauce. Make sure to reserve some cheese for the final layer.
Cover the baking dish with aluminum foil and bake in the preheated oven for 25 minutes.
Remove the foil and sprinkle the remaining cheese on top. Return the casserole to the oven and bake for an additional 10 minutes, or until the cheese is melted and bubbly.
Remove from the oven and let it cool slightly before serving.
Garnish with freshly chopped parsley.
Serve the Lasagna Casserole warm and enjoy!
Note: You can customize the recipe by adding layers of cooked vegetables, such as spinach or mushrooms, between the noodles and sauce. Feel free to add some grated Parmesan cheese on top for added flavor. Let the casserole cool for a few minutes before serving to avoid any burns.

Quick Chili Mac

Ingredients:

8 ounces elbow macaroni
1 tablespoon olive oil
1 pound ground beef (or ground turkey or plant-based ground meat substitute)
1 small onion, diced
2 cloves garlic, minced
1 can (15 ounces) kidney beans, drained and rinsed
1 can (14.5 ounces) diced tomatoes
1 can (8 ounces) tomato sauce
1 tablespoon chili powder
1/2 teaspoon cumin
Salt and pepper to taste
Shredded cheddar cheese (optional, for topping)
Chopped green onions or fresh cilantro (for garnish)

Instructions:

Cook the elbow macaroni according to the package instructions until al dente. Drain and set aside.
In a large skillet, heat the olive oil over medium heat. Add the diced onion and minced garlic, and sauté until fragrant and translucent.
Add the ground beef to the skillet and cook until browned and cooked through. If using plant-based ground meat substitute, follow the package instructions for cooking.
Drain any excess grease from the skillet if necessary.
Add the kidney beans, diced tomatoes, tomato sauce, chili powder, cumin, salt, and pepper to the skillet. Stir to combine all the ingredients.
Reduce the heat to low and let the chili mixture simmer for about 10 minutes, allowing the flavors to meld together.
Add the cooked elbow macaroni to the skillet and stir until the pasta is well coated with the chili sauce.
Cook for an additional 2-3 minutes to heat the pasta through.
Optional: Sprinkle shredded cheddar cheese on top of the chili mac and cover the skillet for a minute or two to melt the cheese.
Remove from heat and garnish with chopped green onions or fresh cilantro.
Serve the Quick Chili Mac warm and enjoy!
Note: You can adjust the spiciness of the dish by adding more or less chili powder. If your child prefers milder flavors, you can omit or reduce the amount of chili powder and cumin. Feel free to customize the recipe by adding diced bell peppers, corn, or any other vegetables your child enjoys.

Cheesy Chicken & Broccoli Orzo

Ingredients:

8 ounces orzo pasta
1 tablespoon olive oil
1 pound boneless, skinless chicken breasts, cut into small pieces
2 cups broccoli florets
1 clove garlic, minced
1 cup chicken broth
1 cup milk (dairy or plant-based)
1 cup shredded cheddar cheese
Salt and pepper to taste

Instructions:

Cook the orzo pasta according to the package instructions until al dente. Drain and set aside.
In a large skillet, heat the olive oil over medium heat. Add the chicken pieces and cook until they are browned and cooked through.
Remove the chicken from the skillet and set it aside.
In the same skillet, add the broccoli florets and minced garlic. Sauté for a few minutes until the broccoli is tender-crisp.
Add the chicken broth and milk to the skillet, and bring the mixture to a simmer.
Stir in the cooked orzo pasta and cooked chicken pieces.
Sprinkle the shredded cheddar cheese over the mixture and stir until the cheese is melted and the sauce is creamy.
Season with salt and pepper to taste.
Cook for an additional 2-3 minutes, stirring occasionally, to ensure all ingredients are heated through.
Remove from heat and let it cool slightly before serving.
Serve the Cheesy Chicken & Broccoli Orzo warm and enjoy!
Note: You can customize this recipe by adding other vegetables such as diced bell peppers or carrots for added nutrition and flavor. Feel free to adjust the types and amounts of cheese based on your child's taste preferences. If desired, you can sprinkle some grated Parmesan cheese on top for an extra cheesy touch.

Fiesta Ravioli

Ingredients:

16-20 ravioli (your choice of filling)
1 tablespoon olive oil
1/2 pound ground beef (or ground turkey or plant-based ground meat substitute)
1 small onion, diced
1 bell pepper, diced (any color)
1 can (14.5 ounces) diced tomatoes
1 can (8 ounces) tomato sauce
1 teaspoon chili powder
1/2 teaspoon cumin
Salt and pepper to taste
Shredded cheddar cheese (optional, for topping)
Fresh cilantro, chopped (for garnish)

Instructions:

Cook the ravioli according to the package instructions until al dente. Drain and set aside.
In a large skillet, heat the olive oil over medium heat. Add the diced onion and bell pepper, and sauté until they are softened.
Add the ground beef to the skillet and cook until browned and cooked through. If using plant-based ground meat substitute, follow the package instructions for cooking.
Drain any excess grease from the skillet if necessary.
Add the diced tomatoes, tomato sauce, chili powder, cumin, salt, and pepper to the skillet. Stir to combine all the ingredients and let the sauce simmer for about 5 minutes.
Add the cooked ravioli to the skillet and gently toss to coat the ravioli with the sauce.
Cook for an additional 2-3 minutes to heat the ravioli through.
Optional: Sprinkle shredded cheddar cheese on top of the fiesta ravioli and cover the skillet for a minute or two to melt the cheese.
Remove from heat and garnish with freshly chopped cilantro.
Serve the Fiesta Ravioli warm and enjoy!
Note: You can customize this recipe by adding additional vegetables such as corn, black beans, or diced tomatoes to the skillet for added flavor and nutrition. Adjust the spices and seasonings according to your child's preference. If desired, serve with a side of sour cream or guacamole for a fun twist.

Threaded Spaghetti Hot Dog Bites

Ingredients:

8 ounces spaghetti
4 hot dogs
Cooking oil (for boiling)
Ketchup and mustard (for serving)

Instructions:

Cook the spaghetti according to the package instructions until al dente. Drain and set aside.
While the spaghetti is cooking, prepare the hot dogs by cutting them into bite-sized pieces, about 1 inch long.
Insert a piece of uncooked spaghetti into each hot dog bite. Push it all the way through the hot dog, leaving a small portion of spaghetti sticking out on each end.
In a large pot, bring water to a boil and add a pinch of salt and a little cooking oil to prevent the spaghetti from sticking together.
Carefully place the threaded hot dog bites into the boiling water and cook for about 8-10 minutes, or until the spaghetti is cooked through.
Remove the hot dog bites from the water and drain well.
Serve the Threaded Spaghetti Hot Dog Bites with ketchup and mustard for dipping.
Enjoy the fun and tasty Threaded Spaghetti Hot Dog Bites!
Note: Ensure the hot dog bites are fully cooked and the spaghetti is tender before serving. Young children should be supervised while eating to avoid any potential choking hazards. You can also get creative by using different types of sausages or adding additional toppings such as shredded cheese or diced vegetables. Let the hot dog bites cool slightly before serving to avoid any burns.

BLT Skillet

Ingredients:

8 slices of bacon
1 tablespoon unsalted butter
2 cups cherry tomatoes, halved
2 cups baby spinach leaves
4 large eggs
Salt and pepper to taste
Bread slices, toasted
Mayonnaise (optional)

Instructions:

Cook the bacon in a large skillet over medium heat until crispy. Remove the bacon from the skillet and set it aside on a paper towel-lined plate to drain excess grease. Crumble or chop the bacon into small pieces.
In the same skillet, melt the butter over medium heat.
Add the halved cherry tomatoes to the skillet and cook for about 2-3 minutes until they start to soften.
Add the baby spinach leaves to the skillet and cook for an additional 1-2 minutes until wilted.
Create four small wells in the skillet by pushing the tomatoes and spinach aside. Crack one egg into each well. Season the eggs with salt and pepper.
Cover the skillet and cook for about 3-4 minutes until the eggs reach your desired level of doneness.
While the eggs are cooking, toast the bread slices.
Once the eggs are cooked, remove the skillet from heat.
Place a toasted bread slice on each serving plate. Spread mayonnaise on the bread if desired.
Using a spatula, carefully transfer one egg with a portion of the tomato-spinach mixture onto each bread slice.
Sprinkle the crumbled bacon pieces over the eggs.
Serve the BLT Skillet sandwiches warm and enjoy!
Note: You can customize this recipe by adding avocado slices or shredded cheese on top of the eggs. You can also add other toppings your child enjoys, such as sliced cucumbers or a drizzle of hot sauce. Adjust the seasoning and cooking time of the eggs according to your child's preference.

Country Bacon-Beef Mac and Cheese

Ingredients:

8 ounces elbow macaroni
4 slices bacon, chopped
1/2 pound ground beef
1 small onion, diced
2 cloves garlic, minced
2 tablespoons all-purpose flour
2 cups milk
2 cups shredded cheddar cheese
Salt and pepper to taste
Fresh parsley, chopped (for garnish)

Instructions:

Cook the elbow macaroni according to the package instructions until al dente. Drain and set aside.
In a large skillet, cook the chopped bacon over medium heat until crispy. Remove the bacon from the skillet and set it aside on a paper towel-lined plate to drain excess grease.
In the same skillet, add the ground beef, diced onion, and minced garlic. Cook until the beef is browned and cooked through. Drain any excess grease if necessary.
Sprinkle the flour over the beef and onion mixture in the skillet. Stir well to combine and cook for about 1 minute.
Gradually pour in the milk while stirring continuously to prevent lumps from forming. Continue stirring until the mixture thickens.
Reduce the heat to low and gradually add the shredded cheddar cheese, stirring until the cheese is fully melted and the sauce is smooth.
Season the sauce with salt and pepper to taste.
Add the cooked elbow macaroni to the skillet and stir to coat the pasta with the cheesy beef sauce.
Cook for an additional 2-3 minutes, stirring occasionally, to ensure the flavors are well combined and the macaroni is heated through.
Crumble the cooked bacon and sprinkle it over the mac and cheese.
Remove from heat and garnish with freshly chopped parsley.
Serve the Country Bacon-Beef Mac and Cheese warm and enjoy!
Note: You can customize this recipe by adding cooked vegetables such as peas, corn, or diced tomatoes for added texture and flavor. Adjust the amount of cheese according to your child's preference. For a creamier texture, you can add a little bit of cream or cream cheese to the sauce. Let the mac and cheese cool slightly before serving to avoid any burns.

Slow-Cooker Mac and Cheese

Ingredients:

8 ounces elbow macaroni
2 cups shredded cheddar cheese
1 cup shredded mozzarella cheese
2 cups milk
2 tablespoons unsalted butter
1/4 teaspoon garlic powder
1/4 teaspoon onion powder
Salt and pepper to taste
Optional toppings: cooked bacon bits, chopped green onions, or diced tomatoes

Instructions:

Cook the elbow macaroni according to the package instructions until al dente. Drain and set aside.
In a slow cooker, combine the cooked macaroni, shredded cheddar cheese, shredded mozzarella cheese, milk, unsalted butter, garlic powder, onion powder, salt, and pepper. Stir to combine all the ingredients evenly.
Cover the slow cooker with the lid and cook on low heat for 2-3 hours, or until the cheese is melted and the macaroni is tender. Stir the mixture occasionally during cooking to prevent sticking.
Once the mac and cheese is cooked and the cheese is fully melted, give it a final stir to combine all the ingredients smoothly.
Taste and adjust the seasoning with salt and pepper, if needed.
Serve the slow-cooker mac and cheese warm. If desired, you can sprinkle cooked bacon bits, chopped green onions, or diced tomatoes on top for added flavor and texture.
Enjoy the creamy and cheesy Slow-Cooker Mac and Cheese!
Note: You can customize this recipe by adding other shredded cheeses or mix-ins such as diced cooked ham, cooked peas, or roasted red peppers. You can also experiment with different spices and herbs to suit your child's taste preferences. Make sure to keep an eye on the slow cooker during the cooking process to prevent the mac and cheese from overcooking or drying out.

Pretty Penne Ham Skillet

Ingredients:

8 ounces penne pasta
1 tablespoon olive oil
1 cup cooked ham, diced
1 small onion, diced
1 bell pepper, diced (any color)
1 can (14.5 ounces) diced tomatoes
1 can (8 ounces) tomato sauce
1 teaspoon dried basil
1/2 teaspoon dried oregano
Salt and pepper to taste
1 cup shredded mozzarella cheese
Fresh parsley, chopped (for garnish)

Instructions:

Cook the penne pasta according to the package instructions until al dente. Drain and set aside.
In a large skillet, heat the olive oil over medium heat. Add the diced onion and bell pepper, and sauté until they are softened.
Add the diced ham to the skillet and cook for a few minutes until it is heated through.
Add the diced tomatoes, tomato sauce, dried basil, dried oregano, salt, and pepper to the skillet. Stir to combine all the ingredients and let the sauce simmer for about 5 minutes.
Add the cooked penne pasta to the skillet and stir to coat the pasta with the sauce and ham mixture.
Cook for an additional 2-3 minutes to heat the pasta through.
Sprinkle the shredded mozzarella cheese over the skillet, cover it, and let it cook for a minute or two until the cheese is melted and gooey.
Remove from heat and garnish with freshly chopped parsley.
Serve the Pretty Penne Ham Skillet warm and enjoy!
Note: You can customize this recipe by adding cooked vegetables such as diced zucchini, spinach, or peas to the skillet for added nutrition and flavor. Feel free to adjust the types and amounts of cheese based on your child's taste preferences. For a tangy twist, you can sprinkle some grated Parmesan cheese on top before serving. Let the skillet cool for a few minutes before serving to avoid any burns.

Salmon Pasta

Ingredients:

8 ounces pasta (such as fusilli or penne)
1 tablespoon olive oil
1 small onion, finely chopped
2 cloves garlic, minced
1 cup cooked salmon, flaked
1/2 cup frozen peas
1/2 cup cherry tomatoes, halved
1/2 cup vegetable or chicken broth
1/4 cup heavy cream (optional)
1 tablespoon lemon juice
Salt and pepper to taste
Fresh dill or parsley, chopped (for garnish)

Instructions:

Cook the pasta according to the package instructions until al dente. Drain and set aside.
In a large skillet, heat the olive oil over medium heat. Add the chopped onion and minced garlic. Sauté until the onion becomes translucent and fragrant.
Add the flaked cooked salmon, frozen peas, and cherry tomatoes to the skillet. Cook for a few minutes until the peas are heated through and the tomatoes start to soften.
Pour the vegetable or chicken broth into the skillet. Bring to a simmer and let it cook for about 3-4 minutes, allowing the flavors to meld together.
If desired, add the heavy cream to the skillet and stir to combine. Cook for an additional minute.
Stir in the lemon juice and season the sauce with salt and pepper to taste.
Add the cooked pasta to the skillet and toss gently until the pasta is coated with the sauce and the ingredients are evenly distributed.
Serve the Salmon Pasta warm, garnished with fresh dill or parsley for added freshness and flavor. Enjoy the delicious and nutritious Salmon Pasta!
Note: You can customize this recipe by adding other vegetables such as spinach or bell peppers to the skillet. Adjust the seasoning and lemon juice according to your child's taste preferences. Feel free to substitute the heavy cream with a lighter option such as half-and-half or milk. Let the pasta cool slightly before serving to avoid any burns.

Chicken Pesto Meatballs

Ingredients:

1 pound ground chicken
1/4 cup breadcrumbs
1/4 cup grated Parmesan cheese
1/4 cup pesto sauce
1/4 teaspoon garlic powder
1/4 teaspoon onion powder
1/4 teaspoon salt
1/8 teaspoon black pepper
Cooking spray or olive oil for greasing
Marinara sauce for serving (optional)
Fresh basil leaves, chopped (for garnish)

Instructions:

Preheat the oven to 400°F (200°C) and line a baking sheet with parchment paper or lightly grease it with cooking spray or olive oil.
In a large mixing bowl, combine the ground chicken, breadcrumbs, grated Parmesan cheese, pesto sauce, garlic powder, onion powder, salt, and black pepper. Mix well until all the ingredients are evenly combined.
Roll the mixture into small meatballs, about 1 inch in diameter, and place them on the prepared baking sheet.
Bake the meatballs in the preheated oven for about 15-18 minutes, or until they are cooked through and reach an internal temperature of 165°F (74°C).
Remove the meatballs from the oven and let them cool slightly.
Serve the chicken pesto meatballs on their own as a tasty protein-packed snack, or toss them in marinara sauce for a saucy option.
Garnish with freshly chopped basil leaves for added freshness and flavor.
Enjoy the delicious and flavorful Chicken Pesto Meatballs!
Note: You can customize this recipe by adding diced sun-dried tomatoes, chopped spinach, or shredded mozzarella cheese to the meatball mixture for extra flavor and texture. Feel free to adjust the seasoning and pesto sauce amount according to your child's taste preferences. Serve the meatballs with pasta, in a sandwich, or as a topping for pizza for a fun twist.

Stovetop Beef and Shells

Ingredients:

8 ounces small shell pasta
1 pound ground beef
1 small onion, diced
2 cloves garlic, minced
1 can (14.5 ounces) diced tomatoes
1 can (8 ounces) tomato sauce
1 teaspoon dried oregano
1 teaspoon dried basil
Salt and pepper to taste
1 cup shredded cheddar cheese
Fresh parsley, chopped (for garnish

Instructions:

Cook the shell pasta according to the package instructions until al dente. Drain and set aside.
In a large skillet, cook the ground beef over medium heat until browned. Break it up into small pieces with a spoon or spatula as it cooks.
Add the diced onion and minced garlic to the skillet with the ground beef. Sauté until the onion is translucent and fragrant.
Drain any excess grease from the skillet if necessary.
Stir in the diced tomatoes, tomato sauce, dried oregano, dried basil, salt, and pepper. Mix well to combine all the ingredients.
Reduce the heat to low and let the mixture simmer for about 10 minutes, allowing the flavors to meld together.
Add the cooked shell pasta to the skillet and stir to coat the pasta with the beef and tomato sauce.
Cook for an additional 2-3 minutes to heat the pasta through.
Sprinkle the shredded cheddar cheese over the beef and shells, and cover the skillet for a minute or two until the cheese is melted and bubbly.
Remove from heat and garnish with freshly chopped parsley.
Serve the Stovetop Beef and Shells warm and enjoy!
Note: You can customize this recipe by adding vegetables such as diced bell peppers or sliced mushrooms to the skillet along with the onion and garlic. Feel free to adjust the seasoning and spices according to your child's taste preferences. For an extra creamy touch, you can stir in a few tablespoons of cream cheese or sour cream at the end of cooking. Let the dish cool slightly before serving to avoid any burns.

Buttered Noodles

Ingredients:

8 ounces egg noodles
2 tablespoons unsalted butter
Salt, to taste
Optional toppings: grated Parmesan cheese, chopped parsley

Instructions:

Cook the egg noodles according to the package instructions until al dente. Drain and set aside.
In a large saucepan, melt the butter over low heat.
Add the cooked and drained noodles to the saucepan with the melted butter.
Toss the noodles gently with the butter until they are evenly coated.
Sprinkle salt over the noodles and toss again to distribute the seasoning.
Taste the noodles and adjust the amount of salt, if desired.
Optional: Sprinkle grated Parmesan cheese over the buttered noodles for added flavor.
Optional: Garnish with chopped parsley for a pop of freshness and color.
Serve the Buttered Noodles warm as a simple and satisfying dish.
Enjoy the comforting and delicious Buttered Noodles!
Note: This recipe is intentionally basic to cater to young palates. Feel free to add other seasonings or herbs if your child prefers more flavor. You can also incorporate cooked vegetables such as peas, carrots, or broccoli into the dish to make it more nutritious and colorful. Let the noodles cool slightly before serving to avoid any burns.

Broccoli Pesto Pasta

Ingredients:

8 ounces pasta (such as penne or fusilli)
2 cups broccoli florets
1/4 cup pesto sauce
2 tablespoons grated Parmesan cheese
Salt and pepper to taste
Optional toppings: cherry tomatoes (halved), grated Parmesan cheese

Instructions:

Cook the pasta according to the package instructions until al dente. Drain and set aside.
Steam the broccoli florets until tender. You can use a steamer basket or cook them in boiling water for about 5 minutes. Drain and set aside.
In a large mixing bowl, combine the cooked pasta, steamed broccoli florets, and pesto sauce. Toss gently until the pasta and broccoli are coated with the pesto sauce.
Add grated Parmesan cheese to the bowl and toss again to combine.
Taste and season with salt and pepper as desired.
Optional: Add halved cherry tomatoes to the pasta for a burst of freshness and color.
Optional: Sprinkle additional grated Parmesan cheese on top before serving.
Serve the Broccoli Pesto Pasta warm as a nutritious and flavorful meal.
Enjoy the delicious and vibrant Broccoli Pesto Pasta!
Note: You can customize this recipe by adding other vegetables such as sliced bell peppers or zucchini to the pasta. Feel free to adjust the amount of pesto sauce and Parmesan cheese according to your child's taste preferences. You can also experiment with different types of pasta for variety. Let the pasta cool slightly before serving to avoid any burns.

Chicken Bacon Ranch Pasta

Ingredients:

8 ounces pasta (such as penne or rotini)
2 slices bacon, cooked and crumbled
1 cup cooked chicken breast, diced
1/2 cup ranch dressing
1/4 cup grated Parmesan cheese
1/4 cup chopped fresh parsley (optional)
Salt and pepper to taste

Instructions:

Cook the pasta according to the package instructions until al dente. Drain and set aside.
In a large skillet, cook the bacon until crispy. Remove from the skillet, crumble, and set aside.
In the same skillet, add the cooked and diced chicken breast. Cook for a few minutes to warm it up.
Add the cooked pasta to the skillet with the chicken.
Pour the ranch dressing over the pasta and chicken. Toss gently to coat the pasta and chicken with the dressing.
Sprinkle the crumbled bacon and grated Parmesan cheese over the pasta mixture.
Season with salt and pepper to taste.
Optional: Sprinkle chopped fresh parsley over the top for added freshness and flavor.
Serve the Chicken Bacon Ranch Pasta warm and enjoy!
Feel free to serve with a side salad or steamed vegetables for a complete meal.
Note: You can customize this recipe by adding cooked vegetables such as broccoli florets, sliced cherry tomatoes, or sautéed bell peppers to the pasta. Feel free to adjust the amount of ranch dressing and Parmesan cheese according to your child's taste preferences. For a creamier version, you can mix in some softened cream cheese or sour cream. Let the pasta cool slightly before serving to avoid any burns.

Spaghetti Tacos

Ingredients:

8 ounces spaghetti
1 cup marinara sauce
1/2 teaspoon dried oregano
1/2 teaspoon dried basil
Salt and pepper to taste
8 taco shells (hard or soft)
Optional toppings: shredded cheese, diced tomatoes, chopped lettuce, grated Parmesan cheese

Instructions:

Cook the spaghetti according to the package instructions until al dente. Drain and set aside.
In a saucepan, heat the marinara sauce over medium heat. Stir in the dried oregano and dried basil. Season with salt and pepper to taste. Let the sauce simmer for a few minutes to warm it up and allow the flavors to meld together.
Add the cooked spaghetti to the saucepan with the marinara sauce. Toss the spaghetti gently until it is evenly coated with the sauce.
Warm the taco shells according to the package instructions, if needed.
Fill each taco shell with a generous portion of the spaghetti mixture.
Optional: Add your favorite toppings such as shredded cheese, diced tomatoes, chopped lettuce, or grated Parmesan cheese.
Serve the Spaghetti Tacos immediately while they are still warm and crispy.
Enjoy the delicious and unique Spaghetti Tacos!
Note: You can customize this recipe by adding other toppings such as sliced olives, chopped bell peppers, or even a dollop of sour cream. Feel free to adjust the amount of sauce and seasonings according to your child's taste preferences. Soft taco shells work well for younger children who prefer a less crunchy texture. Let the tacos cool slightly before serving to avoid any burns.

Simple Tomato Spaghetti

Ingredients:

8 ounces spaghetti
2 tablespoons olive oil
3 cloves garlic, minced
1 can (14.5 ounces) diced tomatoes
1 teaspoon dried basil
1 teaspoon dried oregano
1/2 teaspoon sugar
Salt and pepper to taste
Grated Parmesan cheese (optional)
Fresh basil leaves, chopped (for garnish)

Instructions:

Cook the spaghetti according to the package instructions until al dente. Drain and set aside.
In a large skillet, heat the olive oil over medium heat. Add the minced garlic and sauté for about 1 minute, until fragrant.
Add the diced tomatoes (including the juice from the can) to the skillet. Stir in the dried basil, dried oregano, sugar, salt, and pepper. Mix well to combine.
Reduce the heat to low and let the sauce simmer for about 10-15 minutes, stirring occasionally, to allow the flavors to meld together and the sauce to thicken slightly.
Taste the sauce and adjust the seasoning with salt and pepper, if needed.
Add the cooked spaghetti to the skillet and toss it with the tomato sauce until well coated.
Cook for an additional 1-2 minutes to ensure the spaghetti is heated through.
Remove from heat and garnish with freshly chopped basil leaves.
Serve the Simple Tomato Spaghetti as is, or sprinkle grated Parmesan cheese on top for an extra savory touch.
Enjoy the delicious and straightforward Simple Tomato Spaghetti!
Note: You can customize this recipe by adding cooked vegetables such as sautéed mushrooms, diced bell peppers, or steamed broccoli to the skillet along with the tomato sauce. For a protein boost, you can also add cooked chicken or shrimp. Feel free to experiment with different herbs and spices to suit your child's taste preferences. Let the spaghetti cool slightly before serving to avoid any burns.

I want to take a moment to express my heartfelt gratitude for your recent purchase of my recipe book. As a passionate food lover, nothing makes me happier than sharing my favorite recipes with others. Your decision to invest in my book not only supports my dream, but also shows your commitment to expanding your culinary horizons.

I sincerely hope that the recipes in the book will inspire you to try new things and add some excitement to your meals.

Thank you again for your support and for being a part of this journey with me. I hope my book will bring you many happy and delicious moments in the kitchen.

www.ingramcontent.com/pod-product-compliance
Lightning Source LLC
Chambersburg PA
CBHW081236080526

44587CB00022B/3954